# Kate & Pippin's Family

## The Unlikely Love Story Continues

Martin Springett

Photographs by Isobel Springett

BPS books
Toronto & New York
www.bpsbooks.com

WITHDRAWN FROM
RAPIDES PARISH LIBRARY

RAPIDES PARISH LIBRARY
ALEXANDRIA, LOUISIANA

**K**ate the Great Dane and Pippin
the deer became like mother and
daughter after Pippin was rescued as
a little fawn by Kate's owner, Isobel.
Kate and Isobel looked after Pippin
and made sure she went back to the
forest to live out her life as a wild
deer. But Pippin often visited and
played with Kate.

**P**ippin grew up and had fawns of her own. Isobel and Kate knew they were somewhere in the forest, but where?

Kate and Isobel spent many hours searching for them. Isobel always had her camera with her to take pictures. Pippin had hidden her babies very well, though: They were nowhere to be found. Every little fawn needs its mother to protect it from the many dangers of the forest. Pippin had found a very special hiding place for her young ones.

sobel began to worry that she would never find Pippin's fawns. She and Kate ventured deeper and deeper into the forest, leaving the well-marked trails behind. Isobel was relying on Kate's amazing nose to help sniff out the fawns.

One day Kate and Isobel caught a glimpse of a little fawn, but was it Pippin's? It was gone in an instant.

A few weeks later, Pippin suddenly appeared at Isobel and Kate's house with her twin fawns. Looking for them had felt like a game of hide and seek to Isobel. She decided to name them Heidi and Zeke.

The two fawns were no longer tiny babies, but still they stayed close to their mother's side as they fed on leaves and berries at the edge of the forest.

**K**ate and Isobel were very happy to see Pippin and her new family. Pippin had survived another hard winter in the forest. Not only that, but here she was with two bright-eyed youngsters.

**P**ippin, Heidi and Zeke came to visit every day. They fed together, then walked down to the water-hole near Isobel and Kate's house to drink.

Kate kept a watchful eye on them from the garden surrounding the house. Isobel wondered if Pippin would bring the fawns over to meet Kate. How would they get along?

**P**ippin still liked to get the occasional snack from Richard, Isobel's husband, when she and her family came to visit. Heidi and Zeke stayed well away from Kate, though. Perhaps they were thinking, "Who's that weird deer Mom is hanging out with?" Kate was smart enough to know not to get too close to the fawns. Her special bond was with Pippin.

**H**enry the cat and Kate were getting used to Pippin coming by with her young fawns. Heidi and Zeke usually stayed in the forest while their mom grazed on the lawn around the house.

**P**ippin had to get used to a new member of Kate's family – another Great Dane, this one called Koda. It took a few weeks of careful sniffing and getting to know each other. But after a while Koda and Pippin were hanging out together, too.

Pippin never mistook Koda for Kate, though. She knew exactly who her mom was!

Pippin still liked to visit Henry and give him a bath with her long pink tongue. Deer like salt licks, so perhaps Henry is a salty cat!

Kate and Pippin played together while Heidi and Zeke fed and drank at the water-hole.

**H**eidi and Zeke grew up quickly. Young deer become quite independent of their mothers within a few months of their birth. The twins were content to be together, letting Pippin visit with Kate.

Even though she had two fawns of her own now, just hanging out with Kate was still very important to Pippin.

**P**ippin still loved to play with Kate, just as she did when she was a little fawn, having fun while learning about the world from her adoptive mom.

The next summer, Kate and Pippin were happy when Zeke met a younger sister at the edge of the forest. Pippin had brought her two new fawns to the water-hole to meet everyone.

Isobel called Pippin's new offspring Flora and Fauna. As usual, Kate watched from a distance and was very careful not to scare the little ones away.

Even after four years, Pippin still visited her mom almost every day. Kate was now a grandmother, though she never had pups of her own. Her adopted daughter, Pippin, had thrived in the wild forest and now had a family – Kate and Pippin's unlikely family.

*Dedicated to all orphans, everywhere*
  – Martin and Isobel

Text copyright © 2014 by Martin Springett

Photographs copyright © 2014 by Isobel Springett

All rights reserved. No part of this publication
may be reproduced or transmitted in any form or
by any means, electronic or mechanical, including
photocopying, recording, or any information
storage and retrieval system, without permission
in writing from the publisher.

Published in 2014 by
BPS Books
Toronto and New York
www.bpsbooks.com
A division of Bastian Publishing Services Ltd.

ISBN 978-1-927483-93-0 (paperback)
ISBN 978-1-927483-94-7 (ePDF)
ISBN 978-1-927483-95-4 (ePUB)

Cataloguing-in-Publication Data available from
Library and Archives Canada.

Book design: Martin Springett / Daniel Crack,
Kinetics Design www.kdbooks.ca

CPSIA information can be obtained at www.ICGtesting.com
Printed in the USA
LVIW01n1439291215
468269LV00017B/92

* 9 7 8 1 9 2 7 4 8 3 9 3 0 *